A CENTURY *of*
PAISLEY

This is the design, originating in India, that became known as the Paisley Pattern. The skill of the Paisley weavers and the shawls they created using the Indian pattern made it known worldwide. The new Renfrewshire Council, which includes Paisley in its boundaries, is proud to use it as their logo.

A CENTURY *of* PAISLEY

ELLEN FARMER MBE AND
OLD PAISLEY SOCIETY

First published in the United Kingdom in 2002 by
Sutton Publishing Limited exclusively for
WHSmith, Greenbridge Road, Swindon SN3 3LD

British Library Cataloguing in Publication Data
A catalogue record for this book is available from the British Library.

ISBN 0-7509-3112-4

Illustrations

Front endpaper: Anchor Mills, Paisley, 1960.
Back endpaper: The town from the roof of Coats Memorial Church.
Half title page: Mary Stewart aged thirteen, dressed to attend the Half-timers School Ball before leaving school to work full time in Ferguslie Mills, 1880s. Mary's daughter said her mother was so proud of the fact that she had been chosen by Mr James Coats to lead off the first dance of the evening. *(Paisley Thread Mill Museum)*
Title page: Paisley's old Municipal Buildings decorated for the coronation of George VI, 1937. These buildings were knocked down in the late 1960s to make way for a car park and shopping centre.

Typeset in 11/14pt Photina and produced by
Sutton Publishing Limited, Phoenix Mill,
Thrupp, Stroud, Gloucestershire GL5 2BU.
Printed and bound in England by
J.H. Haynes & Co. Ltd, Sparkford.

Interior of a grocers shop in St James Street, mid-1930s.

Contents

Two adventurous young women on their Raleigh Motorcycle, 1930s. No doubt they would have raised a few eyebrows in their day!

Foreword
by Douglas Alexander MP

In the late nineteenth century, Benjamin Disraeli famously wrote that people should 'keep an eye on Paisley'. In fact, many had been doing just that over earlier centuries – and as a town we continued to attract attention even as we reached the millennium.

It is therefore very fitting that this new book should allow a contemporary audience to turn its eye on Paisley during the years 1900 to 2000. These years saw the illumination of patterns of life established in very much earlier eras and also it was these years which gave rise to much that has contributed to the modern and developing place we know as Paisley today.

A glance back to early and medieval times reveals a Paisley which was a place of pilgrimage. St Mirin of Celtic lore, later the Cluniac Order and finally the majestic Abbey of the Middle Ages gave Paisley a rich ecclesiastical heritage. The positioning and the re-positioning of the Abbey in the town's life and in its landscape is an intriguing narrative and the last century is a graphic chapter of it. The 'religious times' featured early Scottish royalty yet gradually life was changing in Paisley.

Douglas Alexander MP.

Less quiet, less rural and with the beginnings of the industrial transformation of the town, the second half of the eighteenth century was a productive period of Paisley's past. These were 'the silken times' and some of today's street names serve as vivid reminders of the source of the town's wealth: Mill Street, Thread Street, Cotton Street, Gauze Street and Silk Street itself.

The nineteenth century witnessed the arrival of the massive textile mills. These 'textile times' brought to the fore the famous names of Clark and Coats and the intricate elegance of the world-famous Paisley shawl. These years also saw the start of the tradition of 'the mill girls', still fondly remembered to this day.

More recently still have come the great and dramatic changes of the twentieth century – Paisley in the century of two world wars; in the time of railways and then airport runways; in the time of the early radicals and chartists giving way to liberals and to red Clydesiders; heavy industry giving way to service industries and high technology. These more recent times were already reaching towards being 'the technological times' of a new pulsating Paisley.

The span of this book brings into close focus the remarkably formative years of 1900 to 2000 in Paisley's story. A story of changing times, evolving patterns and of people who are proud to belong to a town typical of much that is best in Scotland and its own story over the centuries.

As a native of Renfrewshire and as the MP for Paisley South, I am deeply honoured to represent the people of this place in the parliament of the United Kingdom. A place of ecclesiastical heritage; of industrial pedigree; of historic mills and of a burgeoning modernity. A people of dignity, determination and humour who have seen Paisley through the good days and the bad down the centuries. I invite you to share this most recent account of our doings and developments as we go forward together into the new century. 'Keep your eye on these pages' – and come and visit us to see for yourself!

Introduction

At the turn of the twentieth century Paisley was the largest town in Scotland and industry was at its heart. Names that were known throughout the world started here – Brown & Polson cornflour, Robertson's jam, and Coats and Clarks, the threadmakers, all had their beginnings in Paisley. Shipbuilding and engineering works were also part of the industry that made this a thriving town. However, the thread manufacturers dominated by far.

The huge mills employed around 10,000 people, mainly women. Their working conditions were second to none in the West of Scotland. The factories were almost self-contained in as much as they had their own fire brigade and health centres for the workers. There was a theatre for the Ferguslie Mills drama group, football parks, tennis courts and bowling greens.

Weaving had developed as one of Paisley's main industries in the eighteenth and nineteenth centuries producing silk, cotton and, of course, the beautiful Paisley shawls. Alongside the weaving trade ran many small thread factories, competing with the Coats and Clark families. These smaller firms eventually went out of business or were absorbed into the two big companies. The impact of the textile industry was reflected in the names of many Paisley streets – Cotton Street, Thread Street, Silk Street, Incle Street, Gauze Street, Lawn Street and Shuttle Street.

The great thread manufacturers endowed Paisley with many fine buildings including Paisley Museum, Coats Memorial Church, the George A. Clark Town Hall and the Fountain Gardens. Paisley owed its prosperity to the giant thread mills and when they eventually closed (the last in 1992), it seemed as though the town's prosperity went with them.

However, one of the recent positive developments in Paisley is that we have revisited the history that was virtually forgotten in the days of the great industries. We are learning, and appreciating, the value of our town and helping with its regeneration. Part of this process was the opening of the Old Paisley Society's Sma' Shot Museum.

A sma' shot was a binding thread, usually cotton, essential in the weaving of a Paisley shawl. This small fine thread bound all the others together and occurred every eighth row. It was never seen when the shawl was completed, and the manufacturers did not want to pay for it as they did for all the other threads. But the weavers fought hard and eventually won payment. They marched through Paisley to the beat of the Charleston Drum to celebrate and as a result, from 1856 the first Saturday in July became a holiday known as Sma' Shot Saturday. This was a holiday unique to Paisley and was only removed from the statute book after regionalisation in 1976.

At the start of the twentieth century most people lived in tenement houses which were very overcrowded. One of the many changes that has transformed Paisley in the past

The Half-timers School was built by Coats to give its workers some education before they entered the mill full time. At this time educating girls was a low priority so young girls were considered fortunate to attend. When schooling became compulsory, the building was used for various activities including a dining hall. In time it was sold and became a nightclub. However, in recent years it has suffered various fires and storms and is now in a ruinous condition. It is hoped that it will be rescued and have a future.

hundred years is the expansion of the town outwards to create better housing conditions. This building programme meant losing a great deal of countryside but we are still in the position of having country parks for Paisley people's enjoyment. Muirshiel Country Park was created in the 1970s and Glennifer in the 1980s.

While moving to better housing gave the town's inhabitants the opportunity to improve and enhance their lives, it also meant an end to the days when large families lived together in the same building. In earlier times when a house went empty in a tenement or street, a grannie or auntie would give a good word about another member of the family to the private landlord. It was common for four or five families to occupy whole buildings or streets. There was no need to employ a babysitter because you were never far away from a relative to babysit for you! However, the new housing estates began to develop new communities, and neighbours became almost like family. The new spacious housing also improved the health and welfare of the people who lived on the estates.

Like many other towns in the early twentieth century, Paisley was almost self-sufficient. People did not have to travel far to work as factories were dotted all over the town and included the Glennifer and Isdale & McCallum Soap Works, small food and weaving factories, large and small engineering works and several important shipbuilding firms. The town even had its own part of the car industry – Arrol Johnston.

In the early decades of the twentieth century several events in the town led to significant developments that affected people in Paisley and beyond. On New Year's Eve 1929 seventy-one children died in the Glen Cinema – not in a fire as was first thought, but in the panic that resulted when a film canister started to smoke. After the investigation into the incident, new laws were introduced affecting all public buildings in Britain to ensure such a tragedy could not happen again. For many years the people of Paisley found it difficult to welcome in the New Year in the traditional Scottish style. It left a scar on the town for a long time.

Then in 1932 came a change in the law that affected not just Britain but the whole of the Commonwealth. Mrs May Donoghue from Glasgow had come to Paisley on the evening of 26 August 1928 with a friend. They went to the Wellmeadow Café for an ice-cream and ginger beer. In her ginger beer Mrs Donoghue found a snail! Unfortunately, there was no Consumer Association at that time to help her. She tried to sue the café owner and the manufacturer of the ginger beer, David Stevenson of Glen Lane in Paisley, but had no luck. Then a lawyer in Glasgow took up her case and it went all the way to the House of Lords. As a direct result of Mrs Donoghue's persistence the first consumer law went on to the statute book in 1932. In 1990 a conference was held in Paisley with lawyers and judges from all over the world, including the Lord Chancellor, Lord Mackay of Clashfern. As part of the event a procession was led to the site of the Wellmeadow Café

Paisley Burgh Police being inspected by the Provost of Paisley, 1936.

15

Gilmour Street Station, opened in 1841, was the first of several to serve Paisley. Unfortunately, there are only four left now.

where a bench donated by the University of British Columbia and a plaque were unveiled commemorating the case.

Over the past century Paisley, like other towns, has changed a great deal. Our ancestors of a hundred years ago would find it difficult to recognise their town today. Whole streets have disappeared and much of the countryside they knew is now covered in housing; there is virtually no industry left in the town. However, those people of a century ago would also see healthier children and adults, and some of the diseases they feared have gone. There are wider streets, cleaner air and new buildings.

Glasgow airport is situated within the town's boundaries and has brought thousands of jobs to the area. The large mills have not all been given over to housing. Some are having a new lease of life by being refurbished and restored for use as a business centre, attracting new firms and new jobs to the town. A section of one of the old mills is to be turned over to a new museum celebrating the lives of the thousands of people who worked over a period of 150 years in the thread mills right up until the last one closed in 1992. In addition, the old skills of the Paisley weavers are now playing a part in bringing tourists to see the collection at Paisley Museum. Their ability to work silk and muslin helped create the famous Paisley shawl, and the shawls are valued worldwide for their beauty.

Paisley also has a thriving university. This has its roots in our history as the School of Art and Design and was built in 1848 in Gilmour Street. It was later renamed Paisley Technical College and now, of course, it is the University of Paisley. The university has brought thousands of students to the town from all over the world, creating a new vibrancy. In addition, several new high technology firms have arrived, helping this former mill town to be successful again.

So as Benjamin Disraeli – and Douglas Alexander MP – said, 'Keep your eye on Paisley.' You never know what might come along next.

A Peaceful Beginning, 1900–09

Paisley Cross at the corner of High Street and Moss Street, early twentieth century. The buildings may have changed over the centuries but the cross itself has not altered since Paisley was created a Burgh of Barony in 1488. The Cross has always been the place where people gathered in times of sadness, for example, after the Glen Cinema disaster and the bombing of the Woodside First Aid Post. In happier times people gathered here to celebrate royal visits and the local football team's cup wins.

Women at the weaving mill in George Street, 1900. Some of the women in this picture are really quite elderly but this was in the days before the state pension and some people had no choice but to work well into old age. The old machinery and its overhead belts look dangerous and almost certainly resulted in accidents.

Sma' Shot Day, 1900. The mill band and workers gathered at the end of George Street to walk to the station or bus terminal from where they would depart on an outing to celebrate the annual Sma' Shot Day holiday. This holiday was always held on the first Saturday in July and was unique to Paisley. It remained an annual holiday until Paisley became part of Renfrew District Council in 1976.

Swan the Baker's delivery cart, early twentieth century. Swan's was one of many Paisley bakeries owned and run by local families. Bread was made three times a day and was always available.

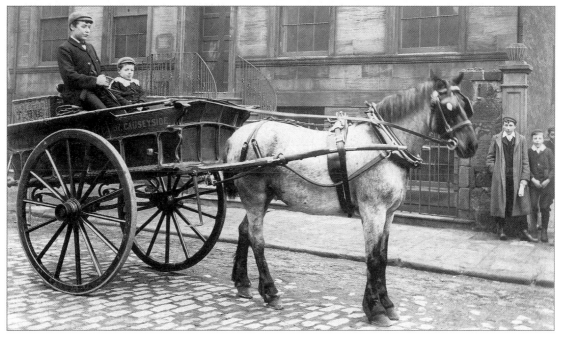

A horse and cart delivering Ure's groceries to customers, another example of local business in towns throughout Britain at this time. No fridges or freezers were available so people had to shop almost every day and small firms gave a good service. Today if you want food delivered to your door you switch on your PC and order it on the Internet!

The Nurses' Home. The Royal Alexandra Infirmary replaced the old Bridge Street Hospital in 1905 and greatly improved conditions for patients in the town. It was built long before there was a National Health Service and funds had to be raised to construct it. Fêtes were held and one Saturday a year was designated Hospital Saturday when the townspeople organised many events to raise money. The Coats family made many contributions, including funding the building of the Nurses' Home.

These girls worked in the spinning department of Ferguslie Mills in about 1910. Although they had bare feet, they also had beautiful hairstyles – they wanted to look their best for the photographer. At its peak Ferguslie Mills employed 5,000 women and in comparison to other mills in the country they were very well paid. *(Paisley Thread Mill Museum)*

Coats Dining Hall, Ferguslie Mills, 1912. This was quite an innovation in its time because many working men and women had to carry food to their place of work or go home for dinner. Mill owners subsidised canteens where workers could have a plain nourishing meal cheaply.

St Mirren FC was, and still is, Paisley's local football team. The club was a founder member of the Scottish Football League and was formed in 1877. Supporters of St Mirren have to be hardy, patient and full of hope as the prizes are few and far between – but when they come the town parties. This was the team for the 1907/8 season.

Paisley Rowing Club was one of the many outdoor clubs that existed before the days of television. There were clubs for all tastes – rambling, bowling, cycling, harriers, curling – all pursuits that people enjoyed in the little spare time they had. Many people worked long hours and getting outdoors was important to them.

Priorscroft Bowling Club, *c.* 1910. This is one of many bowling clubs still going strong in Paisley today. However, it must be far more enjoyable nowadays because members don't have to dress quite as formally as they did then . . . and they allow women to play as well!

A church outing to the Glennifer Braes with everyone wearing their Sunday best clothes, *c.* 1900. The Glennifer Braes has always been a place for outings and still is today. Outdoor concerts were held here every year to celebrate the birth of Paisley's poet, Robert Tannahill. Crowds of many thousands would walk, take charabancs or carts to attend.

This group of well-dressed ladies is typical of the period when a photograph was an important part of family life. Everyone liked to show off how well dressed they and their friends and family were. No doubt dress at work was more modest and practical, but when the occasion arose style and quality were important whatever your place in society.

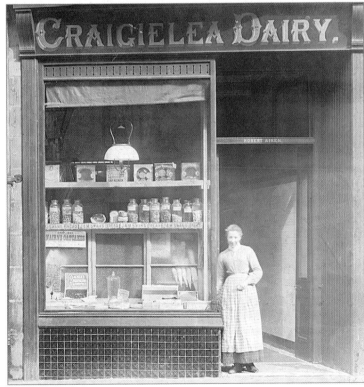

Craigielea Dairy in Paisley was a small family business which, like many dairies in the early twentieth century, had byres in the back where the owners would milk their own cows. This was true even if the shop was close to the town centre. Times and standards of health and hygiene have, of course, changed all that.

Jenny's Well laundry was well known in south-east Paisley. It operated well into the twentieth century. The area is now a small nature reserve which local people and wildlife enjoy.

Well-dressed boys at Ferguslie School, 1910. The school bordered the Coats estate which meant it benefited from various donations from the Coats family, for example, an extra large playground. Many of the children would have been the sons and daughters of families who either worked for the Coats family or were tenant farmers.

The buildings in this photograph from about 1900 have been replaced by the wonderful architecture of the Paisley YMCA building. New Street was a narrow early eighteenth-century thoroughfare which was widened at the beginning of the twentieth century. At that time it was also intended to widen the High Street but fortunately, due to lack of money, this plan was shelved. Luckily, therefore, we still have most of our Victorian High Street intact.

One of many blacksmith shops which abounded in Paisley at the beginning of the twentieth century. When a photographer arrived, it was such a novelty that a crowd would gather, especially children. To the right of the photograph can be seen the end of the old South School. The 'smiddy' became a garage, adapting to the changes of the new modern world. A butcher then occupied the front of the building which was later demolished and replaced.

Queen Victoria's statue, Dunn Square. After Victoria's death in 1901 towns throughout Britain rushed to honour her memory and Paisley was no exception. Sixteenth- and seventeenth-century houses, shops and warehouses had occupied Dunn Square but because they were so close to the river they had been prone to flooding and Paisley's MP at that time, Sir William Dunn, decided to purchase the land, have the square laid out and gift it to the town.

Troubled World Ahead, 1910–19

Peter Craig (dressed as an Indian), Lily Porter and her brother Matt in fancy dress collecting money to help the wounded horses of the First World War. This war was the last time that horses were used in great numbers and it is touching that when so many human lives were lost, people were still able to give a thought to the animals and donate money to rehabilitate them.

In these modern days of small industrial units it is difficult to imagine the sheer size of Paisley's large mills. This picture shows the Ferguslie Mills' own fire engine in 1912. Anchor Mills at the opposite end of the town also had their own fire engine. Both were manned by the mills' own employees. A thread mill on fire would have been a terrifying sight, but fortunately a large-scale blaze never happened.

The Ferguslie Mills Band was well known in the town. All its members were millworkers and their instruments were supplied by their employers. They played for charity events all over the town, and on the first Saturday in July (Sma' Shot Day) they marched through the streets to waken the millworkers for their annual trip away to either the coast or countryside. Stories have it that they played Tannahill's 'O Are Ye Sleepin' Maggie'.

Mrs McKean and her daughters Sybil and Winnie, 1912. The picture was taken during a prize-giving ceremony at the Grammar School, which was established in 1576 by a royal charter from King James VI and is Paisley's oldest school. The school has moved several times in the intervening 400 years and is now in the East End of the town.

Grammar School hockey team, 1918. This was, and still is, a popular game for girls. These girls look relaxed and sedate, but no doubt they wouldn't be so serene when they were on the hockey field. The Grammar School also had an excellent rugby team and a well-known amateur dramatic society.

St Mirren Football Club, Scottish League Victory Cup winners, 1918/19. They went on to win the Scottish Cup three times and still play at St Mirren Football Ground in Love Street. In the early days there would be an average attendance of 20,000 at each game; unfortunately nowadays the fans do not attend in such large numbers.

This is one of a series of glass slides taken of buildings and workers at Ferguslie Mills in 1912. This is No. 1 Spinning Mill, which was one of the largest buildings on the site and was considered to be one of the finest mill buildings in Europe. It was pulled down in the early 1990s and the site is now a housing estate. The last of the Ferguslie Mills closed in 1983.

The engine room at Ferguslie Mills. It looks more like a palace with the beautiful mosaics on the floor, ceiling and walls. This was the room that supplied the energy to run the machines and lighting to No. 1 Spinning Mill. It would have been an awe-inspiring sight.

Women at Underwood Weaving Mill in the early part of the century. As the name suggests the mill was in Underwood Road and was a cloth-weaving mill that specialised in tartans and plaids. The conditions and wages were not as good for these women as for those who worked in the large thread mills, but they were highly skilled workers. The mill closed in the early 1950s.

Paisley Cross has changed a great deal since this photograph was taken between 1910 and 1920. Buildings have come and gone but despite all that, it is still the centre of the town.

The West End of the town looking towards Broomlands and Sandholes Street, *c.* 1910. The building in the centre of the picture is locally known as the Coffin End, the shape of the building explaining the nickname. This was one of the main weaving areas and at one time there were hundreds of weavers' cottages in this part of the town. They were demolished in the 1950s and '60s to make way for street widening and new buildings.

McGeorge tea room and bakers in Paisley. This was a well-known family tea room in the town, one of many run by local people. These families took an interest in the town's politics, many of them being elected as Independent Councillors in the old Paisley Burgh and active in running the town.

This view of Old Sneddon Street shows the condition of some of the housing in Paisley just before the First World War. The picture is clearly dated 1912 and is an example of very good photography of that period. However, it reveals the need for improvement for this part of the town.

The same houses in Old Sneddon showing the back court. The people and the children smile for the camera, but they don't look as if they have much to smile about. They would have had no water or toilets, but they did have a roof of sorts over their head. This kind of picture persuaded those in authority to act: not much later in the century Old Sneddon was pulled down and this area improved.

Private Edward Farmer, his wife Ellen and family photographed when he was home on leave from the First World War. Many families had portraits taken during this period. Edward is with his children, Edward, Robert, Ellen and Elizabeth. He was one of the lucky ones who survived the war. *(Eric Farmer)*

A grand wedding in the Loggia Room at Paisley Town Hall. This building was paid for by George A. Clark, a member of the thread-making family. It was, and still is, one of the finest buildings in the town. It was not an administrative building for the Town Council but was intended for the use of the people of Paisley. When it opened in 1882 there was a public reading room for working men which was open until midnight. It is still a well-used building for weddings, concerts and other activities.

High Church, *c.* 1915. This was the second church to be built in Paisley after the Reformation. Several men died in accidents during its construction and to remember them a pair of spectacles and a handkerchief were shaped in the little cobblestones on the pavement. Generations of Paisley children still walk up School Wynd to look at the memorial. The High Church was renamed when it joined with other churches in the town and is now known as Oakshaw Trinity.

A group of mill girls working at their machines in Ferguslie Mills, 1912. Although the mills had a good record for safety it would be hard to imagine being allowed to work today with your hair hanging down your back. On some occasions, however, accidents did happen and stories of girls having their hair caught in machinery are well known.

John Street, West End. Note the cottage with the thatched roof. Most of the buildings in this street still stand but over the years they have been restored and modernised. It was close to here that the old town gate was situated.

A Decade with A Sad End, 1920–29

A mother and child sitting at the coal fire range. We are now in the 1920s and there is a gas hob connected to the range. However, the fire is still lit to heat the room. The house itself would probably have a bedroom as well as a kitchen. The toilet would be outside and shared with other families.

The workforce of Walter McGee's engineering works proudly posing for the photographer, 12 July 1922. This was one of the many small firms that were situated close to the town centre. In those days most men worked within walking distance of their homes, or close enough for wives or children to take food to them. There was not much commuting then.

The Burgh's carters, one sitting with his dog, 2 September 1926. They were a hardy and strong bunch of men who had their own 'cairter corner' in St Mirren Football Ground, which was the rowdiest part of the terrace! Even today the ground has an area known as Carters' Corner.

This shop stands in the North End of the town at the corner of Love Street and Albion Street and is now a grocers. In earlier times it was a retail and wholesale ironmongers. In the 1920s Paisley was like a series of villages and whatever end of the town you lived – North, South, East or West – almost anything you required could be bought within a short distance of home.

These ladies took part in the Paisley Pageant in 1929. They are proudly dressed in Victorian clothes and wearing the beautiful Paisley shawl. The pageant took weeks to prepare and schools, churches and clubs were all involved. Each organisation was proud to be numbered among the Paisley Buddies and the pageant featured all parts of the town's history, from the monks of Paisley Abbey to William Wallace and the Stewart kings. The Stewart dynasty actually started in Paisley with Walter the High Steward of Scotland and his wife Marjory Bruce, daughter of Robert the Bruce. Marjory and Walter's son became Robert II of Scotland.

On Hospital Saturday, which was an annual event to raise money for the town's hospitals, parades and floats went through the streets collecting money. This 1929 float was named 'A Wagon Load of Mischief' and was mainly filled with mill girls. *(Edward Farmer)*

Young footballers of Mossvale School in the 1921/22 season. Almost all schools had their own teams and played in the inter-school league. Competition between the schools was fierce and when they played it was serious stuff for the boys' parents and teachers. Each school had its own colours and the boys took great pride in wearing them.

Allison the butcher, 1920s. This was one of the best-known butcher shops in Paisley and was owned by the same family for many years. It was eventually taken over by Watson and was in operation until 2001. It was a big shock and a sad day for the town when it closed.

This vessel, named the *Volo*, was built in 1920 by Bow & McLachlan, one of several shipbuilding firms in Paisley. Now, of course, they are all gone. Bow & McLachlan specialised in kit boats which were built, taken to pieces, transported to inland waterways and lakes and then rebuilt.

The *Volo* was built for Mr William Bow of Priory Park. The same firm built her engine, which was quite unusual in those days. With the crew and other staff, this would be an expensive ship to run.

Inside the *Volo*. The men who built these ships were highly skilled – even the engines had to be built in sections to be assembled again on site. The ship was a very handsome vessel, 160 feet in length and 125 feet on the waterline.

Workers from Swan the Bakers posing beside their finished product, 1925. Freshly made bread was the norm in 1925 and there was no chance of GM wheat or any preservatives. If bread was more than a day old it was termed a 'cutting loaf' and you paid less for it.

A group of mill girls on a visit to a photographers wearing their best clothes, 1920s. Because the girls earned good wages for that time they were noted for the fashions they wore and were very conscious of style and what was up to date. At work they had to be more practical – in some departments the cotton flew all over, getting into hair and clothes and sometimes the girls looked as though they had been out in the snow. When work was finished, out came the fashionable outfits.

The Russell Institute is one of the finest Art Deco buildings in Paisley. J.S. Steel Maitland, one of the town's best-known architects, designed it; he was also responsible for Arnotts Department Store and Kelvin House. It is situated at the corner of New Street and Causeyside Street. The building, which was commissioned by the Misses Russell in memory of their brother, was intended as a state-of-the-art clinic for mothers and children. It was opened in 1927 by HRH the Princess Mary. Over the past seventy-nine years many Paisley children will have memories of their visits to the clinic, probably not all pleasant, especially when they were visiting the dentist or having inoculations. It is still in use and serving the purpose it was designed for. *(Sadie Turnbull)*

McDonald's Well at the Glennifer Braes. The well taps a natural spring and was built in memory of Hugh McDonald, a well-known poet and writer who enjoyed walking around the countryside near Paisley. Every year the Tannahill McDonald Club visits McDonald's Well to pay tribute to the poet and his writings. On the well is inscribed the poem 'The Bonnie Wee Well at the Briest O' the Brae' which is well known to Paisley people.

> The bonnie wee well on the breist o' the brae,
> Where the hare steals in the gloamin' sae gray
> Where the wild moorlan' birds dip their nebs and tak' wing
> And the lark weets his whistle ere mounting to sing.

On 31 December 1929 a tragedy happened that no one in the town would forget. It was New Year's Eve and on that day women throughout Scotland gave their homes the traditional cleaning in preparation for celebrating Hogmanay. There was a film matinee at the Glen Cinema so the children went off to enjoy themselves while their mothers carried on with the chores. In the projection room a can of film started to smoulder and smoke filtered through to the auditorium. The children panicked and tried to escape, but the doors were locked. They trampled over each other. Some were smothered by the bodies piling at the door and some were crushed. In all, seventy-one children died that New Year's Eve. *(Daily Record)*

The picture above was taken recently and shows the interior of the Glen Cinema. The building is still intact but partitioned and is now used as a furniture store. Many people in the town think that it was demolished, but a few partitions and some modern fittings are all that covers the building where this major accident occurred. After the inquiry which was held into the tragedy, laws were passed to ensure that an event like this could never happen again. Many restrictions were passed into law: for example, all doors in public buildings must open outward and must not be locked during performances. The children who tragically died in the Glen Cinema have left a legacy that has helped save many lives. The Scottish Film Council erected a plaque to mark the cinema and the part it played in making all cinemas, theatres and public buildings safer. Paisley actor Tom Conti (right) returned to the town to unveil the plaque. (*Paisley Daily Express*)

Opposite, bottom:
The funeral procession was heartbreaking: some families had lost several children and for many life could never be the same again. There was hardly a family in Paisley who was not touched in one way or another by this tragic event. In Scotland it is traditional in most towns to gather to bring in the New Year. However, it was many years before this traditional gathering would take place at Paisley Cross again. (*Daily Record*)

These are the two plaques outside the Glen Cinema, one from the Scottish Film Council and one erected many years ago by Renfrew District Council. Before it was a picture hall, this building was owned by the Good Templars who used it for concerts and soirées in the nineteenth century. It would be a fine thing if money could be found to return it to its original use: apart from bringing about the restoration of a beautiful building, making it a happy place again would be a fitting memorial to the children who lost their lives. (*Paisley Daily Express*)

The 1930s and Britain's First Consumer Law

This couple, photographed in the 1930s, are standing outside the Old Paisley Prison which was demolished in the early 1970s. In later years it was mainly used as the headquarters of Paisley Burgh Police and it was a familiar sight to see officers marching out at the start of a shift. The building had an exercise yard on the roof and its own condemned cell, which, of course, was not used in the building's last hundred years! (After 1868 all death sentences were carried out in Glasgow.) It is now the site of a shopping mall.

DONOGHUE V STEVENSON: MOST FAMOUS CASE OF ALL TIME

The case of Donoghue v Stevenson arose out of an incident on 26 August 1928 at the Wellmeadow Café, 1 Wellmeadow Street, Paisley. Mrs May Donoghue of Glasgow claimed that when refilling her glass from the bottled ginger beer, she saw the partly decomposed remains of a snail. She said she suffered gastro-enteritis as a result of having already consumed some of the ginger beer. Because the ginger beer had been ordered for her by a friend she had no contract on which she could sue. She sued the manufacturer, David Stevenson of Glen Lane, Paisley, claiming that he owed her a duty of care outside the law of contract. Giving judgement in her favour in the House of Lords in 1932, Lord Atkin said he doubted that a more important question had ever come before the House. In a 3–2 decision he held that everyone has a duty to take reasonable care not to cause their 'neighbour' foreseeable harm, defining 'neighbour' simply as any person the defendant ought to have had in mind when committing the act or omission in question. This principle became the basis of the modern 'law of negligence'.

In 1990 the Canadian Bar Association organised a conference about the case of Donoghue v Stevenson. It was more than two years in the planning and this is the procession, which was led by the Lord Chancellor's car, heading for the site of the Wellmeadow Café. The conference was named 'A Pilgrimage to Paisley' and over 300 judges and lawyers attended from Canada, Australia and the UK. The law has been applied in many countries and in thousands of cases involving almost every sort of damage. Donoghue v Stevenson has become known around the Commonwealth common law world as the most famous case of all time.

Paisley Town Hall where the conference was held. Many prominent lawyers and judges presented papers on the case and one year later a textbook for law students was published based on the conference papers. Renfrewshire Council held a wonderful dinner in honour of the delegates and of course snails were on the menu! *(Jack Huberman)*

Lord Chancellor Mackay of Clashfern (second from left) at a reception in the Coats Memorial Church, 1990. He is sitting on a bench that was later placed at the site of the demolished café. The bench is made from Canadian cedar wood and was donated by the University of British Columbia. The reception was held prior to the dedication of the bench and a plaque was also mounted, marking the case and its significant place in British law. *(Jack Huberman)*

The Hon Mr Justice M. Taylor from Vancouver became fascinated with the case and the people involved in it. He contacted the Old Paisley Society to ask for information on David Stevenson, the firm which made the ginger beer, and Mr Minghella the café owner. The society managed to track down Mr Minghella's son, grandson and great-grandson who attended some of the events at the conference. Many people were involved in the gathering which took around two years to prepare, but Justice Taylor was the man who enthusiastically propelled it forward and brought so many people to Paisley. *(Jack Huberman)*

Paisley Burgh Band at the steps of the Fountain Gardens, 1930s. This beautiful park was gifted to the town by the Coats family and its centrepiece is a magnificent fountain. There used to be many concerts here, but times have moved on and Sunday afternoon gatherings in the park are a thing of the past.

The Paisley Comrades Orchestra was one of many musical groups in the town in the 1930s. They played at many concerts and those who remember them say they were excellent. There was also a Paisley Men's Choir, who performed well into the twentieth century, dramatic groups like the Paisley Players, who are still performing, and the Old Grammarians, who have folded. Still well to the fore is Paisley Operatic Society.

One of the many Boys Brigade units from the town, 1930s. This was probably the heyday for youth groups including cubs, scouts, brownies and girl guides. These groups gave children the opportunity of enjoying many activities, especially outside. They could have lots of fun, but still be safe as they learned to build campfires and hike in the hills.

These youngsters may have had a train set or other toys, but for the most part improvised and made their own. A set of old wheels and an old tea chest meant you had your own transport. The picture was taken in about 1937 at Blackstoun Oval. *(June Kennedy)*

Over the years the mills received many royal visits. This is the Prince of Wales arriving in the 1930s. He was a bit of a glamour boy and the mill girls would have been thrilled to meet him.

This mill floor is decorated for the coronation of George VI and Queen Elizabeth, who came to the throne after the abdication of Edward VIII in 1936. Coronations then as now were great events in towns all over Britain, and Paisley was no exception. The mill girls entered into the spirit just like everyone else, and would themselves have decorated their place of work with permission from their employers.

Abercorn Street, 1938. Note how clean the street is and how all the houses have beautifully dressed windows. Some housing was really poor and in bad condition at this time, but in other cases the landlords kept their buildings in a good state of repair. There was very little council housing during this period so most people had to depend on renting from private landlords.

Ferguslie Mills, 1930s. There were at least ten mills on this site as well as the fire station, canteens and first aid buildings. At one time 5,000 people were employed here, but nowadays all the mills have been cleared and this site is totally residential with hundreds of houses in a modern estate. Two small Ferguslie buildings remain, the counting house and one of the gatehouses. They are also homes now.

In the 1930s Paisley, like most towns, had tram cars and many people were involved in the running of them. This picture shows Jackie Edmiston in his tram driver's uniform in about 1937 – very smart he looks too. It was a steady job and certainly better than being cooped up all day in a factory. *(June Kennedy)*

Jackie Edmiston with his twin daughters on his bike posing proudly. Being a tram driver and working shifts he would have had a good chance of seeing his children a little more often than men who worked equally long hours but in straight day shifts. With the long hours that men worked in those days most children would be in bed by the time their father came home.
(June Kennedy)

Smith the Butcher's works dance, 1930s. Most firms would hold some kind of event every year for the workers. Depending on the firm it could be a summer outing or a dance, or perhaps even both. These events played an important part in people's social life. Many a romance, some leading to marriage, started at these dances and outings. (*June Kennedy*)

These ladies are taking a break outside their place of work but one of them is still busy with her knitting. Time was not wasted when it could be used for knitting cardigans or jumpers for the family. When they finished their day's work they would be off home to cook the family meal and do the housework before they could even think of relaxing.

Preparing for war with sandbags and of course an Anderson shelter, 1939. People could still enjoy the sunshine in the garden, not knowing what was yet to come. *(June Kennedy)*

War and Peace

This photograph comes from the album of a family at war but still
optimistic about the future. They typified families all over Scotland who
carried on as normally as they could in an abnormal world. The women
endured hardship and rationing as the men were away fighting. They had
to feed their children and worked long hours, some in munitions factories
and some in the mills. Men needed uniforms and the hospitals needed
sheets so cloth and thread were in great demand.

Like all towns, Paisley was prepared for any eventuality. First aid posts were constructed and volunteers were recruited to man them. This is a post in George Street but later a new one was built at Woodside. At dawn on 6 May 1941 the Woodside post was bombed and ninety-two people died. There were only four survivors. The bombing was the worst single disaster to hit Scotland during two world wars. The victims are buried in a communal grave in Hawkhead Cemetery. There is a sad footnote to this bombing. Robert McConnell aged eleven perished in the Glen Cinema disaster (see pages 50–2); his sister Mary escaped only to die in Woodside First Aid Post aged twenty-one. *(Paisley Daily Express)*

A remembrance service held at Woodside Crematorium on the sixtieth anniversary of the bombing of the First Aid Post. It was a touching service, especially for two of the survivors who were able to attend, and for the relatives of some of the people who lost their lives. *(Paisley Daily Express)*

GVI RI

HONI SOIT QUI MAL Y PENSE

DIEU ET MON DROIT

This scroll commemorates

H. McKay

Civil Defence Service

held in honour as one who
served King and Country in
the world war of 1939-1945
and gave her life to save
mankind from tyranny. May
her sacrifice help to bring
the peace and freedom for
which she died.

A certificate was sent to a family after their daughter was killed at the first aid post. It is sad to think of all the families over Britain who received similar letters and certificates during the Second World War. Paisley was fortunate during the conflict as bombing was slight compared to places like London, Clydebank and Coventry. However, this would be no comfort to the families of the people who died at Woodside.

King George VI and Queen Elizabeth visiting Anchor Mills, *c.* 1942. They travelled extensively throughout Britain visiting factories and talking to people who were working tirelessly for the war effort. These visits were kept quiet because of security worries. *(Paisley Thread Mill Museum)*

The king and queen visited Ferguslie Mills the same day. You can see by the smiles on the mill girls' faces that they enjoyed the visit. It would have been a welcome break for them. The girls not only worked at the mills but also organised fundraising groups to help the soldiers, sailors and airmen. They knitted for them, they helped out in hospitals and they even raised enough money to buy an aeroplane. Can you imagine the amount of fundraising that would take today? *(Paisley Thread Mill Museum)*

Paisley Burgh Special Constables, 1945. Everyone who could do something for the war effort did. This poem was written by Paisley poet Alexander Barr for War Weapons Week.

Well done Glasgow, and all the rest
For savings week you've done your
   best
Now it's Paisley's turn to show
How keen we are to crush the foe

We've got the men; they've proved
   their worth
In every corner of the earth
Our need today is £.S.D.
Each shilling helps to keep us free.

Our Provost asks a million pounds
Paisley with patriots abounds
If each will save that little more
Above that figure we can soar.

Boys Brigade company of Martyrs' Parish Church, 1945. All the youth movements carried on during the Second World War. In addition to keeping the children busy, they would 'do their bit' to help in many ways to try to ease the burden for people around them.

Many women in the services saw action all over Europe. This is a group of young nurses at a military hospital in Italy in 1945. Nita Devoy from Paisley is in the centre of the back row. These women's task was to nurse the wounded and help them recover enough to be sent back home. *(Nita Devoy)*

Paisley Girls Training Corps at the East School, 1944. It is wonderful how people rally round at a time of crisis. People from all walks of life who might be having difficulties themselves could always find time to help others. *(Jean Goldie)*

Children at South School, 1940s. People treasure these photographs taken so many years ago for the memories they hold and for the people who shared their childhood. Some of the people in this photograph are scattered around the world and some still enjoy life in their hometown. (*Bruce Seaton*)

South School again, but a different class, *c.* 1947. The South School was one of four built when education was made compulsory in the late nineteenth century. It had a slightly different curriculum from other schools in Paisley in that as a third element of their studies pupils could attend a commercial course where extra subjects like shorthand, typing and book-keeping were taught. There were two fee-paying schools in the town during the 1940s, Paisley Grammar and the John Neilson Institution. There were also other senior secondary schools and of course secondary and primary schools. After primary school the 11-plus results determined whether children would go to a senior secondary or basic secondary school. (*June Kennedy*)

Gibson's Tea Room and Bakery was one of Paisley's best-known venues for functions and wedding parties and was situated on a prime site in the High Street. It was built in the Art Deco style, but sadly it is now long gone. A wedding reception on 21 June 1940 was carried out in first-class style. At this time a typical reception at Gibson's consisted of a high tea which included baked fish with Parisian potatoes, cold roast lamb or galantine of chicken, bread, scones, cakes, cut cakes and biscuits. A buffet followed later with lemon cup and ices. Then a hand-round tea with cakes followed towards the finish. The total cost of the foregoing was £9 10s for a minimum of thirty guests and a rate of 5s 6d for each additional guest. The cost of a two-tier wedding cake with one set of pillars, weighing 15–16lb, was £3 3s. Gibson's could also boast that it had a fine electrically amplified music reproducing service which was available, if desired, for bridal and wedding marches, and/or dancing at a cost of 12s 6d for the evening. The Old Paisley Society has a complete library of old-fashioned and modern dances and games from this era.

During the war, most families could only have the occasional day away and it was quite usual for several women in a street to organise day trips. This photograph was taken on a trip to Seamill in 1945. This is the Fergus family and note that casual wear was not the normal code of dress in 1945. Mother is wearing her coat and father his suit and tie. *(Frances Jones)*

The Edmiston family on holiday in Troon, 1940s. This wasn't just a day away; the planning would be meticulous. It was the custom to take a house down the coast and for Paisley families this normally meant Ayrshire. One week before the holiday the big wicker travel hamper would be brought out and packed with everything the family required for their one or two weeks' stay. The hamper would be sent on ahead and if anything was needed before the holiday and it was in the hamper, then tough luck! *(June Kennedy)*

New Developments,
1950–59

Listen with mother, 1950s. Little Susan Reid sits in her family's new prefab home beside the radio. Prefabs were temporary housing put up after the war to help ease the great housing shortage. People loved their prefabs. Susan certainly looks delighted in hers. There are still some left in the town today. *(John and Brenda Reid)*

Barr Street, 1954. These houses were about to be demolished. Paisley Burgh Council, like the councils in most British towns and cities, worked hard in the 1950s to create better housing conditions for the townspeople. Many old houses had to be pulled down but people often did not want to move. Compulsory purchase was then introduced.

A back court, Barr Street, 1954. Wash-houses and outside toilets were shared by several families and normal living conditions could be very bad if a landlord did not carry out the repairs required to keep housing up to standard – and many landlords did not.

This photograph shows new houses going up while some of the old were waiting to be demolished. This is the area around George Street in the town centre. The people who moved into the new houses loved them – and no wonder. There were spacious bedrooms with fitted wardrobes, each house had its own bathroom and kitchen, and best of all, there was no sharing toilets with other people. Folk soon forgot that they hadn't wanted to move!

Paisley's first high-rise flats. Building work started in 1957 and families moved in in 1959. In recent years, flats like this have had a bad press but these ones in George Street are still among the most sought after in the town. The story goes that people moving in to George Street flats are there until they have to be carried out!

The mechanics from Anchor Mill on an outing to Girvan, 1950s. The mill had many special departments and had its own joiners, mechanics, engineers and dyers. However, women were still in the majority by thousands. It was said that Paisley had seven women for every man. Men were considered lucky if they courted a mill girl!

The joiners at Anchor Mill had their own workshop and were on call to do any work that was required around the site. They would build cabinets and cupboards, as well as repair floors and windows, etc. Like most people in the mills they were friends as well as workmates, and would meet together outside the workplace to take part in the activities the mill provided, like bowling and other sports.

Staff at Ferguslie Mills, 1955 or 1956. This is an extract from a poem written by a former mill girl.

Ah remember the days we aw
    worked in the mill
An' a real thrivin' place it was then
The early shift worked fae six tae two
An' the back shift fae two to ten.
    Ah wis four foot ten, in ankle
        socks
    But ah wis sure that ah looked
        classy
    The mornin' ah first left the
        house
    Tae become 'a wee mill lassie'
We fair thought we wur there fur life
We had nae hint o' trouble
So it fairly broke our hearts tae see
Oor mill reduced tae rubble.

(Marion Hernon)

A presentation at Ferguslie Mills, *c.* 1955. In the mills, like other workplaces, if anyone was leaving to get married, emigrating or retiring, there were always colleagues who would have the task of gathering money for the person leaving. In some cases the presentation would be followed by a party of some kind. If it was a marriage there was ritual to observe. On the day the bride was leaving, her coat would be 'confiscated' and decorated with paper flowers and ribbons. At the end of her shift her friends would walk her home through the town singing as they went. *(Marion Hernon)*

School sports were high on the agenda in the 1950s and all schools took part. This is the South School relay team who took part in their own school's sports day and the inter-schools event. This was an important day for all pupils who took part and, indeed, all the schools that participated. *(June Kennedy)*

West School netball team, 1955. The young girls are all posing proudly, knowing they had performed well. It is surprising how well these girls (now adult women) remember the friendships made so long ago during that period of their lives. Nostalgia thrives! *(Frances Jones)*

The Anchor Bar in Gauze Street decorated for the coronation of Queen Elizabeth II in 1953 and for her visit to Paisley the same year. Gauze Street was on the queen's route through the town, so shops, pubs and cafés made sure they were noticed, although on the day of her visit, so many people packed the street that the decorated properties could hardly be seen. *(June Kennedy)*

The interior of the Anchor Bar with manager J. Edmiston, 1953. The bar was locally owned, as were many of the pubs in the 1950s. One well-known pub in Paisley, the Bull Inn, was managed by a woman who was known to run a tight ship. If a man came in for a drink wearing his working clothes, he was served with one pint and then sent home to his family. If he returned washed and changed, he was made welcome. This landlady was definitely not part of the women's liberation movement – she would allow no woman in her pub! *(June Kennedy)*

Street parties were held in almost every street in the town for the coronation. This one was organised in Glen Street and the people here really went to town – they even had a life-size model of the queen. In addition to all the traditional events like games and sing songs, there was of course plenty of food! (*Paisley Daily Express*)

The queen went to many places all over Britain in her coronation year and each town really tried to make her visit special. In Paisley all schools had a holiday so that the children could turn out to wave and cheer. For once, the weather was glorious on the day of her visit. (*June Kennedy*)

Paisley Pirates hockey team, 1955. Paisley had a 5,000-seat ice rink in 1955 and the Paisley Pirates were extremely popular. Almost every game was a sell-out because they were also one of the top teams at this time. *(June Kennedy)*

The Paisley Pirates in action, *c.* 1955. The ice rink played host to other big events, including an exhibition fight by Muhammad Ali, although he was known then as Cassius Clay. Boxing was a regular attraction, as were exhibition matches by the famous Harlem Globetrotters basketball team. There were also tennis tournaments and people turned out in their thousands to watch their favourite sports stars. Unfortunately the site was sold to a supermarket chain. Paisley now has a new ice rink, the Lagoon, but it has a much smaller seating capacity. *(June Kennedy)*

The Royal Highland Show in St James Park, 1950. The park was formerly known as Paisley Racecourse and was used for many years for racing before it closed in 1908. When the Royal Highland Show came to Paisley, the park was one of the largest in the town. On its edge there were tennis courts and bowling greens. The park also held the annual fair which was visited by thousands of Paisley Buddies every year. The fair still turns up every Paisley Fair Week (the first two weeks in August) but is on a much smaller scale because the park is much reduced in size. It is mainly used for football now with many pitches where hundreds of young footballers play out their ambitions to the delight of everyone who watches them. Who knows, we may see some of them play for Scotland one day!

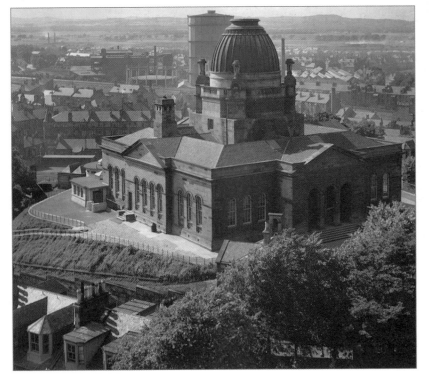

One of the best-known buildings in Paisley is the John Neilson Institution. John Neilson of Paisley endowed it for the education of children in the town. The school was built in 1852 and was designed by architect Charles Wilson. As time went on, the school became overcrowded and more space was needed for the pupils so a new school was built at Ferguslie. The original, beautiful old building, known affectionately by locals as the Porridge Bowl and seen here in the 1950s, lay empty for a few years but has now been converted into flats.

Full Employment,
1960–69

A stairhead toilet at Howard Street. Sharing a toilet was a way of life for many families throughout Scotland, even to the recent past. This one in Howard Street was well looked after and was kept in pristine condition. However, this was not always the case and many an argument was fought in a close if other tenants did not look after the toilet when it was 'their turn'. It was customary to have a key with a tag on it, which you passed on when your turn was finished. In Paisley, of course, it was usually a bobbin, so you 'passed the bobbin'. *(Harry Hornby)*

First Aid Centre at Ferguslie Mills, 1960s. It looks more like a bungalow in India. This was where the millworkers would go with minor injuries or if they were unwell. A doctor visited every week to help the nurses with any problems. It was well equipped and they could deal with almost anything. *(Mima Pratt)*

Coats Mill ambulance, 1960s. Standing beside it is Marion Meikle who served at Coats and Clarks Mills all her working life. The ambulance was always on standby for any emergency and could be relied upon to get you to the Royal Alexandra Infirmary quickly. If staff had any doubt about a patient's health, the patient would be sent to the hospital. *(Mima Pratt)*

Nursing staff at Ferguslie Mills, 1960s. Many former employees of the mills will find these faces familiar. The nurses worked a shift system in keeping with the mills', which meant that whether people were working day shift or late shift, there would always be someone on hand to help if necessary. *(Mima Pratt)*

Many of the men and women thread mill workers were keen bowlers and both Ferguslie and Anchor mills had bowling greens and clubhouse facilities. Bowling was taken seriously. This photograph shows a presentation of a bowling trophy at Anchor Mills in 1960. Some of the trophies were donated by the mill owners and some were funded by the bowlers themselves.

Bonnie Wee Well Tea Room at Glennifer Braes, 1968. This was a welcome place to visit after a long walk over the braes. A walk up the braes was a regular trip for many people in the 1950s and 1960s and still is, but unfortunately the tea room was demolished a number of years ago. There are still fond memories of the welcome tea and sandwiches it provided. *(Harry Hornby)*

Tannahill's Cottage. This thatched cottage was the home of Robert Tannahill (1774–1810), who is sometimes known as Paisley's weaver-poet. His father built him the cottage and Robert lived there until he died by committing suicide. It was said that Robert was suffering from depression at the time. His body was found by his friend Peter Burnett. Peter was a Black man who had escaped from slavery in America and was befriended by Robert's family. The Paisley Burns Club, of which Robert was the first secretary, now owns the cottage. *(Mima Pratt)*

Brian and Brenda Hillcoat and friends with their hand-made cart. You can tell we have reached the 1960s by the name on the cart – The Six Five Special, which was the popular rock'n'roll television programme at that time. Even in the 1960s children were still making their own toys and having great fun with them too. *(May Hillcoat)*

These little girls are all dressed up in their party frocks and standing outside prefabs to have their photograph taken. Inside there would be the usual party treats of that era – birthday cake, sandwiches, cakes, ice-cream and jelly. *(John and Brenda Reid)*

The end of a tennis tournament at Anchor Mills Recreation Ground, 1960s. The grounds had tennis courts and bowling greens and were in the main used by the employees of Clark Mills, but local schools were also allowed to use them for school sports days. When the mills closed in 1992 most of the area was sold off and part of it is now a new housing estate.

This view of the Town Hall with the old Municipal Buildings and prison was taken prior to the redevelopment of the town centre in the 1960s and 1970s. The Town Hall remains the same but almost all the rest is gone, replaced by a modern shopping mall.

Paisley Technical College (founded in 1896) is now part of the University of Paisley. This building is now part of a much larger campus and only one of the many buildings that make up the university. Since it was created in 1992, the university has grown, and because of its success building work is still ongoing to accommodate the students who wish to attend.

One of the first of the new buildings erected as the Technical College started to expand. Many more have been added since then. The University of Paisley also has campuses in Ayr and Dumfries and has around 8,000 students attending its comprehensive courses.

The new Glenburn Housing Estate built by Paisley Burgh Council in the late 1950s and early 1960s. To make way for this estate Paisley Golf Club was resited and several farms removed. The people who moved into these new houses now had a much better standard of living and, for many, their own garden for the first time.

Paisley Cross with still more changes, 1960s. New buildings have been added to the Victorian ones. However, the Cross still keeps its character and is the same shape as it was in medieval times. Returning emigrants visiting the town may see many changes, but Paisley Cross is still a familiar sight (see also pages 17 and 35). *(Andrew Pratt)*

Workers at Seedhill Finishing which was close to the Anchor Mills, 1960s. Viyella cloth was woven here and it was another loss to the town when it closed in the 1970s. Many of the workers had moved here from other cloth or dyeworks factories as they slowly closed over a period of years. They are now all gone. This seems to be the story of manufacturing throughout Britain.

Quality control at Seedhill Finishing Works, 1969. Attention to detail is important when a quality cloth is being woven and workers had to be highly skilled to ensure that quality was maintained. Paisley had a reputation for quality at its best and this reputation still lived on in the Seedhill Finishing Works in the late 1960s.

The mainly Victorian High Street in 1960 before some of the buildings were pulled down and replaced by modern concrete structures – Marks & Spencer, Littlewoods and what used to be a Woolworth's store. Here an ugly window has been installed half way up a Victorian building occupied by John Collier and Richard Shops; surely this window could have been replaced with something more in keeping with the surrounding buildings?

The End of an Era

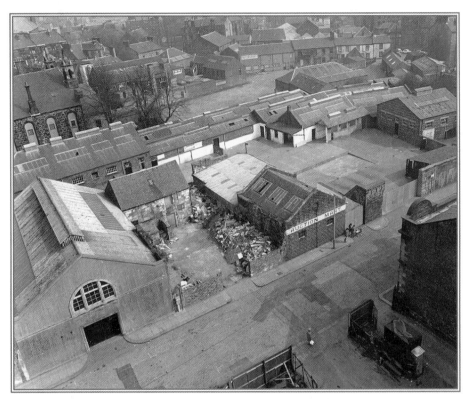

Paisley market when it was located in the town centre, 1975. This was a thriving market but it became impractical to hold a cattle market in the town centre: the days were gone when cattle and sheep could be driven down Paisley High Street! The market has now moved to the outskirts of the town and the University of Paisley has acquired most of this area.

This is a familiar picture to many townspeople, the old Municipal Buildings and prison. They were buildings full of character but were too small for the number of people now required to run local government and were demolished in the early 1970s to make way for a new shopping mall. The local government and new Strathclyde Region offices moved to another part of Paisley.

This is the shopping mall that replaced the old buildings. When it was first built, it was not too popular with many local people, mainly because it was constructed over the River White Cart and people were used to seeing the river running through the town. It now stops abruptly at the Cross and disappears under tons of concrete. However, this area has recently been refurbished and now looks much better. *(Sadie Turnbull)*

Shona and Paul Hornby having fun on the roundabout at East End Park. This park is much smaller now due to the redevelopment of this area of the town in the 1970s. Many of the old tenement properties were demolished and whole streets are now gone. In their place is the new Lagoon Centre with swimming pool and ice rink. The rest of the development comprises the ring road. *(Harry Hornby)*

The newly resited Priorscroft Bowling Club under construction, 1972. Paisley people enjoy their bowling and the town abounds with well-attended, well-run and prosperous clubs. Only those who don't know call it an 'old folks' game. Many young people also enjoy their bowling. *(Harry Hornby)*

A mill girl dressed up by her workmates prior to her marriage, May 1975. The ritual which hadn't changed much over the years finally moved into modern times. No longer did the girl hold a party in her home where her mother would serve sandwiches and cakes and at one point in the evening ask her colleagues 'Would you like a glass of sherry or port?' Now girls take their friends to places like Amsterdam, Dublin and Paris for 'Hen Nights'!

Weddings and retirements were occasions when friends and workers could show how much you were appreciated. They would spend time taking a collection of money to buy a nice gift and then arrange for a celebration on the date you were leaving. These were happy events. If you were retiring, it did not mean the end of contact with friends and colleagues as there were many reunions for outings and dinners.

The Domestic finishing mill at the Anchor site. It has lain empty for many years and looks derelict and vandalised. However, plans are being made by the Phoenix Trust to restore it by creating flats on the upper floors with small business units below. This building is in a prime site in the town centre and the flats will have fantastic views over Paisley and the surrounding countryside.

A sad view of buildings being demolished at Anchor Mills: this has been a familiar sight during the 1980s and '90s. However, some still stand and at least at the Anchor site they will continue to act as a reminder that Paisley was an industrial giant in the past. It is difficult to know what to do with these massive buildings. Some conversions have been successful and work well for the area they are in. Perhaps the Anchor Mills site can be one of them.

Anchor Mills pensioners at their annual gathering, 1980. This is an event much enjoyed by all, with memories and gossip to the fore. Meeting up with old colleagues, and discussing past friends and 'who worked in what department' give a great deal of pleasure to everyone concerned. The mill closed in 1992 but the gathering still takes place every year.

A group of children playing in Cochrane Street. The increase in traffic in town centre areas has almost stopped this kind of activity. Children are largely confined to their own garden or supervised in parks. However, many adults have good memories of playing outside and can recall back-door concerts when they spent many happy hours rehearsing before performing for parents and friends. *(Harry Hornby)*

Andrew Mitchell (right) at a presentation at St Mirren Football ground in Love Street. Young Andrew was being awarded a prize for his entry in an art competition by footballer Frank McDougal. St Mirren Football Club is involved in helping develop youngsters who have an interest in the game, and supports many community activities.

This view shows the old and new side by side – the ancient Abbey of Paisley and the new Municipal Buildings, constructed between 1969 and 1974. The area around the Abbey has recently been refurbished, landscaped and, in the main, pedestrianised. This has improved the appearance of the Abbey and Town Hall for the many thousands of people who visit every year, and for those who live here. (*Sadie Turnbull*)

Alexander Wilson was born in Paisley on 6 July 1766, emigrated to America in 1794 and died in Philadelphia on 23 August 1813. He was the first person to make a comprehensive study of American birds and travelled the length and breadth of America in the early nineteenth century to pursue his studies. His book on American ornithology ran to nine volumes! His statue stands between Paisley Town Hall and Paisley Abbey. He was also an accomplished poet and had a volume of his poetry published in 1789. Paisley has never forgotten him. *(Sadie Turnbull)*

This statue of Robert Tannahill stands in Abbey Close near to Alexander Wilson's. He was well known for his poetry and songs, among them 'The Bonnie Woods of Craigielea', 'Jessie the Flower o' Dunblane' and 'The Braes o' Balquidder'. He was born on 3 June 1774 and died on 17 May 1810 – a short life indeed. In the late nineteenth and early twentieth centuries Tannahill concerts were big social events in Paisley's calendar. Every year they were held in the open air at the Glennifer Braes and thousands of people would attend them. The money raised went to help pay for the statues you see today. *(Sadie Turnbull)*

Changes Ahead

Sma' Shot Cottages Heritage Centre, George Place. Purchased by the Old Paisley Society in 1983, these cottages have since been restored to their original condition by volunteers. Later the society also purchased an original weaver's cottage in Shuttle Street, which was built around 1740. Sma' Shot Cottages reveal the lifestyle of millworkers in the nineteenth century and handloom weavers in the eighteenth century. In just one visit, two periods of history can be explored. The weaver's cottage still has the original looms on display. These were kindly donated by Paisley Museum. The cottages are open to the public and still run by volunteers.

Canal Street Station was built in 1883 and took its name from the old Glasgow–Paisley–Ardrossan Canal, the railway following the line of the filled-in waterway. On a public holiday in 1810 the canal was the scene of a horrific accident when too many people boarded a boat chartered to take them to Glasgow for a day's excursion and it capsized. People on the top deck landed in the canal and eighty-five were drowned, eight of them around eight years old. Many more were teenagers. *(Harry Hornby)*

The station closed in 1983 at a time when the railways were being, as they say in modern language, downsized. There was a lot of protest at the time because many towns and villages lost their stations and had to rely on cars and buses to get to Paisley and Glasgow. The buildings of the old station became a restaurant and bar in 1989 and remain so today. The line has reopened but only from Paisley to Glasgow. *(Harry Hornby)*

This was the fate of No. 1 Spinning Mill at Ferguslie. It was demolished in 1993 after three public enquiries and numerous protests, and the site has now become another housing estate. However, there is still hope that some of Paisley's other thread mills will continue to find new uses. One has already become a business centre and another at Anchor Mills may become luxury flats.

Demolition of Ferguslie Mills chimney, 19 September 1983. The demolition was quite a spectacle and people came from all over to watch it. There is always an element of danger when something like this takes place and there was also a little sadness in seeing a familiar landmark disappear. A use can sometimes be found for an old building, but what do you do with an old chimney? However, one chimney has been classed as a listed building and survives at the Mile End Mill. (Harry Hornby)

Sma' Shot Day was revived in 1986 by Renfrew District Council. Paisley folk singer Danny Kyle was given the job of organising it. Danny, who has since died, had a small but enthusiastic team helping him, but no one knew how successful the event would be after a break of all those years. In older days Sma' Shot Saturday was marked by thousands of people in celebrations and a day's excursion out of the town. Danny's team researched and planned and worked hard to encourage local people to get involved and take part.

The day eventually dawned and many local people were indeed actively involved. They made banners and costumes and Danny insisted that children and adults, from eight-year-olds to pensioners, took part in the parade. After all, in 1856 when Sma' Shot Day was introduced young children worked and so did many people well past pension age. Everyone who was taking part gathered at the Brodie Park. The band was there too and led the parade. But still the organisers worried. Would the public turn out to watch it? Would they patronise almost 100 charity stalls set up in Storie Street where the parade was due to end? Well they did! In their thousands, they lined the route and cheered every band, every banner and everyone in the parade.

One of the weavers' groups who took part in the 1986 Sma' Shot Parade. The original procession was led by the Ferguslie Weavers, followed by those from other areas of the town – Causeyside Weavers, Charleston Weavers and Newton Weavers, etc. The annual parade still takes place in Paisley on the first Saturday in July. It traditionally set off from the Dooslan Stane (Stone) which was taken from its original site at the corner of Rowan Street and Neilston Road and now sits in Brodie Park in Paisley. The Charleston Weavers used the Stane as a platform when they held meetings, and tradition said that whoever stepped on it had the right to be heard by the others present. It was also said that anyone who could get them off the Stane could then take their place and had the right to put their point. There must have been some lively meetings if this was indeed the rule! *(Paisley Daily Express)*

Young Rachel Hall at Sma' Shot Cottages dressed in period costume and wearing a Paisley shawl. The Paisley shawl was not a garment working women could afford. Their husbands may have been responsible for weaving it but it was destined for the luxury market. The nearest women workers got to the Paisley shawl was to crop and finish it for richer people to wear *(Paisley Daily Express)*

The Charleston Drum leads the parade and is a copy of the original drum that can be seen in Paisley Museum. In the days before telephones, cars and public transport the drum was used to let the weavers know where and when meetings would be held. It was carried through the town by two men beating on it and calling out the time and place of the meeting. This usually happened when there was a dispute with the Cork over payment or conditions. The Cork was a slang expression for the master manufacturers. It meant they were 'generally light; or in a commercial sense, without substance, given to airy speculation and floating on the surface of trade'. *(Paisley Daily Express)*

In 1987 St Mirren won the Scottish Cup for the third time. When a local club like St Mirren wins the cup, it is not just football fans who celebrate, but the whole town. Thousands of people – children, adults, grannies and grandads – all celebrated together. The council arranged a civic reception and people crowded around the Cross and Town Hall to see their team arrive. St Mirren don't win this cup very often but when they do, it creates wonderful memories for the whole town. *(Paisley Daily Express)*

In 1488 Abbot Shaw of Paisley Abbey received from King James IV a charter raising the town to the status of a burgh. In 1988 Paisley celebrated 500 years as a burgh and Queen Elizabeth visited as part of the celebrations. There was a special service in Paisley Abbey and she was welcomed by thousands of Paisley Buddies.

Queen Elizabeth also made a special visit to Paisley Museum where she enjoyed looking at the display in the Shawl Gallery. As a memento of her visit, she was presented with a handcrafted silver brooch and a Paisley shawl. While she was in the town she also planted a rose in Dunn Square. Many events took place to celebrate Paisley 500, but Her Majesty's visit was the highlight for many people.

Paisley Museum kindly invited some of the members of the Old Paisley Society to come along on the day of the queen's visit and to wear Victorian gowns and Paisley shawls. It was an experience they will never forget. They designed and made the dresses themselves and as far as they were concerned, it was worth all the weeks of hard work.

Paisley Today

Jenny Kemp at Sma' Shot Cottages holding Paisley's own flower – the dianthus, Paisley Gem. At one time there were 140 varieties of Paisley Pinks. Now this is the only one that can be identified and it is rare. The Beechgrove Garden Hit Squad came to the cottages to change the garden. They found the Paisley Gem in a nursery that preserved old varieties and now it is back in the town. The Paisley weavers loved growing flowers and the Paisley Florist Society is the oldest in Scotland. *(Paisley Daily Express)*

Folk singer Danny Kyle and Sadie Fogg with a Paisley shawl which Danny had brought back from one of his tours to America. It was in a bad condition, and Danny had promised the owner he would find someone to repair it. He did. This is Sadie modelling the shawl she spent months repairing and a grand job she made of it too. Sadly Danny and Sadie died within six months of each other but not before she heard the special verse of Danny's song 'The Music of the Loom' which he had written to thank her for her work in the restoration.

A group of people setting out on a walk around Paisley. In recent years, more and more people are taking an interest in Paisley's history and heritage walks have become very popular. For many older people local history was not a subject taught in schools. It certainly is now in Paisley but adults and children alike are still keen to learn more, and, as can be seen from this picture, they certainly enjoy the walks. *(Paisley Daily Express)*

Celebrations for the fiftieth anniversary of VE Day at Sma' Shot Cottages, 1995. People all over the country celebrated the anniversary of the ending of the war in Europe and had great fun in the process. Some looked out old uniforms, searched out gas masks and uncovered photographs of their parents to see how to dress. The Old Paisley Society had some items that people had donated to the collection so members Brenda Reid and Harry Hornby managed to look the part. In addition to dressing up, Sma' Shot Cottages' volunteers dismantled the nineteenth-century artisans' kitchen and constructed a 1940s room complete with typical 1940s furniture and crockery. There was even a Bakelite radio playing '40s music and a hidden tape playing BBC comedy shows. There was, of course, a street party, which was held in the garden, with plenty of tea and spam sandwiches.

This was one of the town's grandest cinemas. It was named the Picture House and was built complete with a grand restaurant and a fountain playing in the foyer. Cinemas were in their heyday when the Picture House was built in the 1930s on the site of an earlier movie theatre and no expense was spared in its construction. There was also an organ so people could sing along to music. 'Going to the pictures' was at least a weekly habit before the advent of television. This cinema was known to all in Paisley as 'The Old High Street'. *(Harry Hornby)*

When the Picture House closed down in the early 1980s, permission was given to build a shopping centre in its place. The Picture House was demolished and so were many of the buildings in and around the area. However, it was decided that the façade of the cinema would remain, keeping the frontage of the High Street unchanged.

The Fountain Gardens is one of Paisley's finest parks and is named after the beautiful fountain in its centre. Thousands of children have enjoyed the fountain since the park was bought by the Coats thread family and gifted to the town in 1868. Unfortunately the fountain is showing its age and is not running regularly now. It needs extensive repairs to restore it to its former glory. (*Sadie Turnbull*)

Paisley Abbey today. The area around the Abbey has been cleared and landscaped in recent years and now makes a most fitting location for the town's most historic building. In the past few years archaeologists have discovered part of the old Abbey drains and have also found some wonderful artefacts, among them Scotland's earliest written music which is on slate. The River Cart at the Abbey was the site of the first recorded curling match which was played in around 1540. The history of this old Abbey is the history of Paisley. (*Sadie Turnbull*)

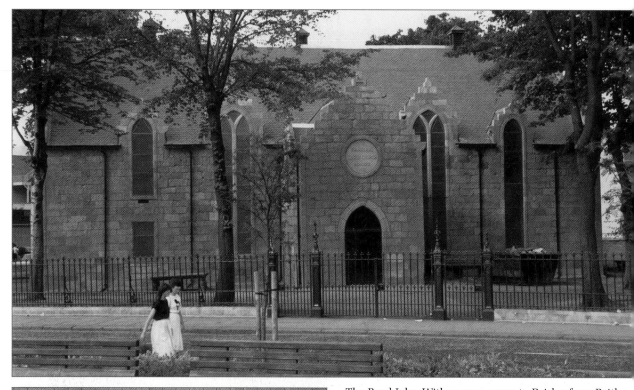

The Revd John Witherspoon came to Paisley from Beith in 1757 to what was then the Laigh Kirk and is now Paisley Art Centre. He was a member of the evangelical movement within the Church of Scotland – the Popular Party, as it was sometimes called. He believed that acting, singing and dancing were wrong for anyone who called themselves a Christian. There is no doubt about how he would react to the news that his former church is now an art centre! He did, however, have some trouble with some of his congregation who felt differently from him. Nevertheless he was a popular preacher and had the support of his church members. He was invited to America by the New Jersey College, now Princeton University, and was elected its president in 1766. *(Bob Durkee, Princeton University)*

This statue of John Witherspoon stands in the grounds of Princeton University. An identical one is sited outside Paisley University. The universities wanted to honour jointly the connection between John Witherspoon and Paisley. The statue at Princeton was unveiled in November 2001 and stands in a beautiful setting within the grounds. *(Bob Durkee, Princeton University)*

The sculptor responsible for both statues is Paisley's Sandy Stoddart. His most recent work was for the queen's new gallery at Buckingham Palace. John Witherspoon was a supporter of the American War of Independence and was the only clergyman to sign the Declaration of Independence. *(Bob Durkee, Princeton University)*

The first Witherspoon statue was erected in Paisley on 22 June 2001. It was unveiled by the Princess Royal, Princess Anne, and stands outside the main entrance to Paisley University. The town has many links with the United States of America and when the second statue was unveiled at Princeton University in November of the same year it reinforced the connections between the two.
(Paisley Daily Express)

The Mile End Mill is one of the few remaining mill buildings in Paisley and fortunately a new use has been found for it so it will have a future. It is now a business centre and as a result is bringing new jobs to the town. No dark satanic mill is this. Paisley folk are pleased to see the building being used and employing people again. *(Ann Dick, Architectural Photographer)*

Part of the Mile End Mill has been given over to a group of people who want to keep alive the memories of the thousands of men and women who worked in this building and other mills in the town. The Paisley Thread Mill Museum is due to open in 2002 and former millworkers are among the people who will play their part as volunteers to keep memories alive for future generations. This photograph shows mill owner Marcus Dean receiving a £1 note from Professor Joe Hendy, Chairman of the Mill Museum, as one year's rent. Paisley South MP Mr Douglas Alexander attended the ceremony. Mr Dean's actions show that benefactors still exist in the town of Paisley today.

Acknowledgements

Thanks to the many people who provided photographs and whose names are acknowledged in the book credits. Thanks also to the Old Paisley Society photographic archives for all the photographs not otherwise credited. A special thanks to Old Paisley Society Secretary, Hazel Lindsay, and Vice-President, Di Adam, for all their assistance in the production of this book.

Ellen Farmer MBE

Detail of the Russell Institute building (see page 48). *(Sadie Turnbull)*